When There
Is a Death

By Sara Appel-Lennon

Illustrated by Magdalena Steimle

ISBN: 979-8-9989712-0-4 (paperback)
ISBN: 979-8-9989712-1-1 (eBook)

First edition 2025.

MAYIM
PUBLISHING

.

I dedicate this book to (CK) Richard John Lennon, my late husband, who was always early. He taught me life continues after death.

Je t'aime!

Sara

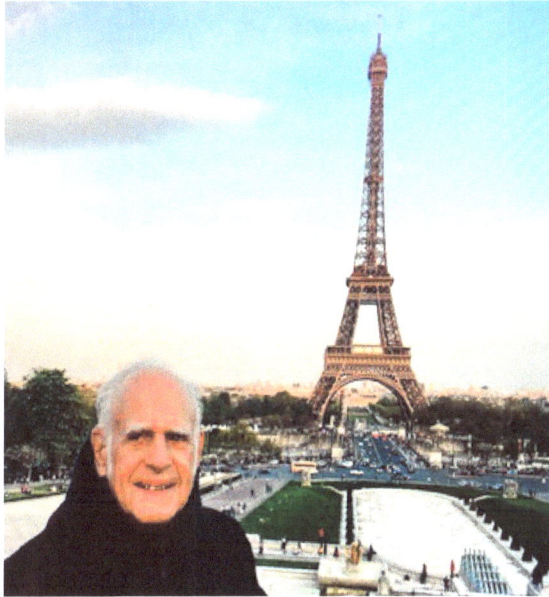

(CK) Richard John Lennon
April 2, 1935 – February 13, 2025
San Diego, California

Retired in 1992 after 32 years at San Diego Gas
& Electric as Employment & Labor Relations
Director.

Started college recruitment program of
engineers.

Richard was third cousin to John Lennon of
The Beatles.

See greenwoodmemorial.com.

Foreword

This book is a quiet companion for when grief arrives.

This tender, illustrated poem offers a gentle shelter—an invitation to breathe through loss, to feel deeply, and to trust that simply being is enough.

In the silence between the words, space opens to honor what the heart holds.

The authenticity of the author's meditation practice gently reveals itself—rooted in the quiet courage to turn toward pain, to be fully present in the moment, and to trust in the art of poetry to offer a kind of holy consolation.

Moira Novack

Author's Note

I wrote this book to give a voice to my grief, after several people in my circle died.

Grief is part of life. You're not alone.

When there is a death, life continues; and you can too, one breath at a time.

Breathe deep. You're still here.

My husband, (CK) Richard, died the evening before Valentine's Day of 2025. We were together for 21 years, married for 19 years.

Best wishes as you heal,

Sara

When There Is a Death

When there is a death,

breathe deep.

You have breath.

Fitting to feel grief;

robbed, toppled by thief.

Life has its sorrow.

Time cannot be borrowed.

Weeping bitter tears;

breathe deep.

You're still here.

Burning, red, hot, mad;

missing what you had.

Lonely, scared, sad, blue;

Faith will see you through.

When there is a death,

breathe deep.

You have breath.

Acknowledgments

I would like to express gratitude to my terrific team:

Brynn Steimle
For her professionalism, communication, and dedication.

Magdalena Steimle
For following my vision and successfully highlighting my poetry with her paintings.

Shelley Voss
For her illustration input.

Thanks to the reviewers for their heartfelt testimonials:

Jolene Brackey, Moira Novack, Jennifer Smith, Nina Tomkiewicz, Jenny Woodworth

And last but not least, I give myself a high five for publishing this book.

Thanks to my grief support team:

Elizabeth Hospice Spousal
Bereavement Thursday group

"Courage to Caregivers" for their
support and compassion

Caregivers' Expressive Writing Group
for their kinship and camaraderie

Friends who stood beside me

About the Author

Sara Appel-Lennon has two bachelor's degrees, a teaching credential, and a feature writing certificate. She completed the Dale Carnegie course and served as a graduate assistant. She was also the recipient of a Picture Book Biography Weekend Intensive Study at the Writing Barn in Austin, Texas.

Sara has written articles for San Diego Society of Children's Book Writers and Illustrators, *The La Jolla Light*, and *The La Mesa Courier*. And she led poetry groups at the San Diego Blind Center and the San Carlos Library. Sara values making a positive difference.

About the Illustrator

Magdalena Steimle has been creating art since she was still in diapers. Her first masterpiece was "Mouse Eating Cheese" at the age of three.

Her paintings have been featured in various shows and she is the recipient of the Linton-Barnhill award.

Magdalena also works in technical theater as a scenic designer and artist.

This is Magdalena's debut as a book illustrator.

Please write a review on Amazon.

I'd love to hear how my book helped you.
I can be contacted at
mayimpublishing@gmail.com.

Thanks for joining me on this journey.

Best wishes,

Sara

www.ingramcontent.com/pod-product-compliance
Lightning Source LLC
Chambersburg PA
CBHW041809040426
42449CB00001B/22